Mexico City

Delaplaine 2019

LONG WEEKEND GUIDE

Andrew Delaplaine

NO BUSINESS HAS PAID A SINGLE PENNY OR GIVEN
<u>ANYTHING</u> TO BE INCLUDED IN THIS BOOK.

A list of the author's other travel guides, as well as his political thrillers
and titles for children, can be found at the end of this book.

Senior Editors – **Renee & Sophie Delaplaine**
Senior Writer – **James Cubby**
Art Director – **Chip McGoldrick**

Gramercy Park Press
New York – London – Paris

Please submit corrections, additions or comments to
andrewdelaplaine@mac.com

MEXICO CITY
The Delaplaine
Long Weekend Guide

TABLE OF CONTENTS

Chapter 1
WHY MEXICO CITY?

I love Mexico City, even though the first time I traveled there, with my mother, we almost brought her back in a box. She had made the mistake of using the ice cubes in her hotel room fridge to make a drink instead of pouring bottled water into the ice trays.

Boom!

You're sick as a dog.

But that was many years ago. Generally, I've had nothing but wonderful times in Mexico City.

When I think about what Mexico City was and how it came to be what it is today, my mind still boggles.

You have to remember that the whole city is built on a drained lake bed. When there was still a lake, around 1325, it was established as the Aztec capital called Tenochititlán. The island in the middle of the lake was reached by way of a series of causeways. This was what Hernan Cortes found when he showed up in 1521. He promptly destroyed it.

Mexico has a rich and bloody history, not unlike all the other countries in the New World where the indigenous populations where slaughtered or enslaved. (But one has to remember that Cortes didn't do anything to the Aztecs that the English settlers didn't do to the Indians.)

The altitude is high, over 7,000 feet, so if you come from a low-lying coastal area, be prepared for some difficulty in breathing. And while the government has made enormous strides in cleaning up the famously polluted air in Mexico City, it's still pretty awful. You have to pray for good air. But you can never be sure of it.

There are things about Mexico in general that you want to be aware of if you want to travel wisely—and safely. The State Department says 14 of the 31 states (and Federal District, or *Distrito Federal*, or D.F., which is Mexico City) have no travel warnings. The others you want to avoid because of the drug-related gang warfare that's an ongoing reality in Mexico, responsible for ripping the country apart. (Americans are really to blame, since we're the ones buying all the drugs.)

One of the reasons Mexico City is so much more safe than other parts of the country is that everybody wants to be able to come here and visit it in peace, and this includes a lot of the high-end drug dealers, many of whom have houses and families here. They don't want to come here and duel it out on the streets the way they do elsewhere.

Of the 20 top foreign locations for Americans, 4 are in Mexico: No. 2 is Cancun, followed by No. 3, Playa del Carmen, Cabo san Lucas / Los Cabos at No. 11 and Puerto Vallarta at No. 15.

One good thing about Mexico City is that it has been sidestepped by the drug cartels so there's no sense of the overwhelming violence that occurs in other parts of Mexico.

You will find the *Distrito Federal* (Federal District, another name for the city) to be quite a beautiful, handsomely laid-out city.

Lay of the Land

At 571 square miles, D.F.—as Mexico City residents, or *chilangos*, call it—is vast, but visitors gravitate to a few key neighborhoods.

Centro Histórico: Anchored by the Zócalo plaza, the historic center is a mix of monuments and bustling commerce.

Roma: Hipsters, artists, and boutique owners have revived this once-bourgeois neighborhood of Art

Nouveau mansions.

Condesa: In Mexico City's answer to New York's West Village, shops, restaurants, and apartments radiate out from the Parque México.

Polanco: One of the city's poshest districts keeps expanding north: "Nuevo Polanco" is being colonized by galleries and shopping malls.

Getting Around Safely: Taxis are plentiful, but you may feel more secure having a private car. From Journey Mexico at www.journeymexico.com

For the latest safety information, go to the U.S. State Department at travel.state.gov.

CASH & DEBIT CARDS.

Notify the companies whose cards you use that you are going to Mexico. Transactions might be blocked if you don't. Have them send you alerts or call you if any charge looks suspicious. When using ATMs, try to avoid street side ATMs in favor of ATMS inside a bank or other business.

Have credit card numbers and other information written down in a safe place.

You'll need cash because a lot of places don't accept plastic. But get your currency converted before going to Mexico because you'll stick out as a foreigner by getting it done at the airport when you land. (The rates are high there too.) A lot of currency exchange booths are not in secure areas, so beware.

YOUR DRESS.

You're not in Vegas, you're in a potentially dangerous city, so leave the shorts and flip-flops at home unless you're visiting the beach somewhere. Don't be an obvious tourist. Keep your camera in your travel bag, not around your neck.

YOUR PHONE.

Don't be glued to it the way so many people are, not when you're out on the streets. You're begging for trouble.

Check with your carrier to find out what the fees are when traveling in Mexico.

TAXIS.

See below.

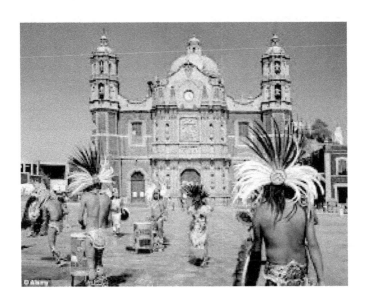

Chapter 2
GETTING ABOUT

There's an extensive Metro system, a bus system, a trolley system. I would avoid them all unless you *really* know your way around. I never use them. Never.

They even have special cars on the Metro system for women only because women get groped on the mixed cars. Also there's the constant threat of pickpockets. Stay away.

Mexico City is one of the world's largest cities and boasts an estimated population of 21 million people living in the region. Mexico City is divided into 16 areas known as delegaciones, not unlike New

York's boroughs. These areas are further divided into neighborhoods called "colonias" and there are about 250 of these.

When traveling the city, it is important to know which colonia that you're traveling to and be aware that some have duplicate or very similar names. Visitors to Mexico City need to take note of the increase in crime and safety concerns that are prevalent in the city.

While traveling throughout Mexico City by public transportation can be economical, it is not always the safest mode of transportation and warnings regarding use of public transportation should be respected.

Locals and those familiar with Mexico City travel freely and cheaply via the Metro, first- and second-class buses.

However, visitors should travel by *sitio taxis* (official taxis registered to a specific locale or hotel), as these taxis are fairly inexpensive and the safest means of travel within the city.

"Turismo" and Sitio Taxis

These two methods are the safest means of travel within Mexico City. Turismo taxis, un-marked cabs, are usually luxury cars that are assigned to specific hotels and are identified by their special license plates. These may be more expensive that other taxis but they are the safest.

Established rates are fixed for travel to and from the airport. However, rates for traveling to other destinations and sightseeing need to be negotiated with the drivers.

The bell captain at your hotel can tell you what the airport fare should be and make sure to confirm with the cab driver before departure. Theses cab drivers, usually licensed English-speaking guides, can be excellent tour guides and provide valuable information regarding Mexico City.

While these cabs usually charge around 15% more than metered rates, the price is well worth it as these drivers can wait for you while you dine or shop or will pick you up when you call.

Getting Around Safely: Taxis are plentiful, but you may feel more secure having a private car. From Journey Mexico at www.journeymexico.com

Metered Taxis

Some sitio taxis (radio taxis) are safe and use meters, others have fixed rates. Travelers need to be cautious as some drivers will overcharge passengers, advance the meter, or even drive farther than requested to run up the tab. One recommended safe radio taxi service is **55 5590 3325** or **55 6898 5192.**

Do not hail a taxi. A lot of the drivers are unlicensed, illegal and unsafe.

Your hotel will call a reputable taxi for you, a "radio taxi." If you're in a restaurant and ready to leave at night, have them call a cab for you.

If you're out on the street and need a cab, go into a nearby hotel or restaurant and have them call for you. Or go to a taxi stand, labeled *Sitio de Taxi,* where real tcxis will be located. These are designated taxis and OK to use. These maroon and gold Nissans are slightly more expensive than the green *libre* taxis, but much more secure.

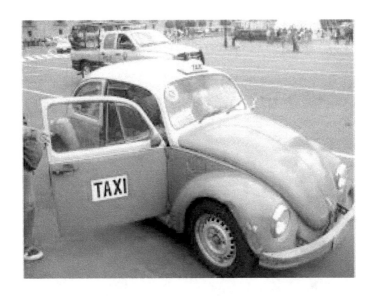

Metro

The Mexico City subway offers one of the cheapest fares in the world and has twelve lines that cover the entire city. The Metro is open Monday – Friday (5 a.m. to midnight), Saturday (6 a.m. to midnight), and Sunday (7 a.m. to midnight). The Metro is very crowded during the day and traveling during rush hours should be avoided. Tickets are sold at the ticket booth in each station. After passing through the turnstile, look for two large signs showing the destinations and follow the signs. Make sure you know where you are going as there is only one map with the routes at the entrance of the station. Note: SALIDA means EXIT and ANDENES means PLATFORMS. Once you get on the train, there's a map of the station stops for that line only located above each door. CORRESPONDENCIAS means transfer points. Be prepared to walk a bit inside the Metro system, especially when transferring lines.

Remember, this is not the safest way to travel and Metro pickpockets prey on tourists.

Bus

Traveling by bus is common for locals. However, visitors should beware. There are bus stops on all the major tourist streets and most post a map with the full route description. The Metrobus, introduced in 2006, runs in its own designated lane up and down Avenida Insurgentes and usually travels faster than the surrounding traffic. Most of these buses are used by commuters but if you know where you're going and know the stop, the Metrobus is a better alternative to the other buses.

Microbuses

Some tourists like to use the peseros (microbuses); these are sedans or minibuses that run along major roadways. These buses have established fares and pick up and let off passengers along the route and usually offer a more comfortable ride and speedy journey. These microbuses are usually green and gray and display cards in the windshield with their routes. As the bus nears a stop, the driver will put his hand out the wind displaying one or more fingers indicating the number of passengers he can accommodate.

Tourist Bus

Many cities feature the red double-decker hop-on and hop-off tour buses (in Mexico City they are called **Turibuses; 55 5133 2488** or www.turibus.com.mx) and here in Mexico City they offer different tours in the north and south of the city. Each bus seats 75 and offers an audio tour in five languages. These buses operate from 9 a.m. to 9 p.m. and for a set fee tourists can hop-on and hop off as often as desired. One of their most popular tours is the Chapultepec-Centro Histórico route with 25 stops including major monuments, museums and neighborhoods. Another favorite circuit takes passengers from La Roma neighborhood south with stops that include the World Trade Center, Plaza de Torros bullring, Carillo Gil museum, Perisur shopping center, and the Frida Kahlo museum. Another tour route goes to the pyramids at Teotihuacán.

Rental Car

If you are traveling without a car and want to travel to Puebla or other surrounding areas, you may consider a rental car. Be warned that due to the high percentage of auto theft, **renting a car in Mexico City is not recommended**.

Do not rent a car unless you're familiar with the area. These people drive like maniacs. The last thing you want is to be in a fender bender in this country where bribes are so common. If you're not prepared to deal with the police, avoid renting a car.

It is not advised to drive in the city if you're not familiar with the streets and neighborhoods, especially if you don't read Spanish, as all the signs are in Spanish, and you certainly don't want to take the chance of landing in one of the city's unsavory neighborhoods. One safe option is to hire a car with a driver—Avis offers chauffeur-driven rental cars at all of its Mexico City locations –the drivers know the area and are great tour guides. (Avis – 800-352-7900 in the U.S. or 1-800-288-8888 in Mexico).

Chapter 3
WHERE TO STAY

CONDESA DF
Avenue Veracruz 102, Col., 52 55 5241-2600
www.condesadf.com/main.html
NEIGHBORHOOD: Condesa
This is definitely one of the top places you will want
to consider staying in because it's new and hip and
attracts a trendy crowd not only as guests, but to its
charming public spaces. Paris designer India Mahdavi

took over this 1920s French Neoclassical style building and jumped it up with turquoise walls and ultra-modern furnishings. The outside of the building is distinguished and stately. Inside, it's a crazy wonderful colorful surprise. They offer 40 rooms arrayed around a courtyard in the center. The place is decorated with alpaca carpets, Oaxacan blankets, dark wood paneling and other fun items. The Condesa neighborhood is home to numerous art galleries and fun, stimulating shops, so this place also makes an excellent stop for a drink after you've done some exploring and shopping. (Get the cucumber mezcal mojito made with mezcal blanco by Los Danzantes of Oaxaca.) If you're visiting in the spring, you'll love the blooming jacaranda trees with purple flowers surrounding the rooftop terrace where there's also a sushi bar. In the basement at night there's a dance club where it goes on till late.

DOWNTOWN MEXICO HOTEL

Isabel La Católica 30, Mexico City, +52 55 5282 2199
www.downtownmexico.com
NEIGHBORHOOD: Downtown/Historical District
This hotel combines Colonial 17th century grandeur with a modern twist. Next to Colonial landmarks on a cobbled street, this hotel is located in the central balcony of the Palace of the Countess of Miravalle. In a unique setting filled with art, guests can enjoy breakfast. The large terrace offers great views of the historic churches, Torre Latinoamericana and the Casino Espanol. The owners, Grupo Habita, have elegantly combined the old structure with modern touches, like the bar and pool on the rooftop that attracts a fun crowd. Be sure to explore the

mezzanine where there are carefully selected shops selling mescal, pottery from the provinces and rich chocolates. Amenities include: Flat screen TVs, Bigelow Apothecaries, dry cleaning, Wi-Fi, and room service.

FOUR SEASONS HOTEL MEXICO, D.F.
Paseo de la Reforma 500, Mexico City, +52 55 5230 1818
www.fourseasons.com/mexico/
NEIGHBORHOOD: Cuauhtémoc
Located near Chapultepec Park, this beautiful hotel has a staff as smooth as any you'll find in any Four Seasons hotel around the world. You get the feel of Colonial times in the lobby and rooms, as well as the courtyard, its fountain offering a soothing respite from the din outside. The hotel offers 240 elegantly appointed guest rooms, including 40 suites. Amenities include: LCD flat-screen TVs, free wireless high-

speed Internet access, heated outdoor pool, spa, and fitness center. On-site restaurant, **Reforma 500**, offers Latin American cuisine and lunch and/or cocktails are available at **El Bar**. Around the corner from the hotel entrance, on Calle Burdeos, you'll find street-side vendors selling really good tacos and other street food.

INTERCONTINENTAL PRESIDENTE MEXICO CITY

Campos Elíseos 218, Polanco, Polanco IV Secc, 11560 Ciudad de México, CDMX, +52 55 5327 7700
www.ihg.com/intercontinental/hotels/gb/en/reservation

NEIGHBORHOOD: Federal District / Polanco

Overlooking Chapultepec Park, this modern high-rise (42 floors) hotel offers 661 guest rooms and suites. From the higher floors you get a magnificent view of the mountains that encircle the city (when the air isn't terribly polluted, which is not often). Depending on your rate, you'll probably get a buffet breakfast included with you room. You'll find it to be heads and shoulders above most such buffets, with eggs made to order, lots of pastries. There are 5 or 6 restaurants on site, including an outpost of New York's steakhouse, the **Palm**, **Chapulin** (serving Mexican cuisine), an import from Paris, the bistro **Au Pied de Cochon**, which actually does a great job of replicating the bistro atmosphere they have in Paris; the trattoria **Alfredo di Roma**, that has a nice outdoor terrace. Once I was here on a whirlwind 4-day trip working on a movie script and the producers put me up here. I was holed up, never able to leave the room except occasionally. I spent time in all these restaurants and was very satisfied. Amenities: Wi-Fi (surcharge), flat-screen TVs, iPod docks and coffeemakers. Hotel facilities: cocktail lounge, health club & spa, ballroom, and indoor swimming pool. Conveniently located near National Museum of Anthropology, Ruth Lechuga Museum and Paseo de la Reforma, which has lots of buses and numerous cabs.

LA CASONA
Durango 280, Cuauhtémoc, Mexico City, +52 55 5286 3001
www.hotellacasona.com.mx
NEIGHBORHOOD: Federal District
With its central location, this small, cozy hotel offers guests 29 exclusive guest rooms. Amenities include: free 10Mb Fibreoptic Internet, flat screen TV with cable, safe deposit boxes, writing desk, room service, air conditioning, and snack basket. No smoking rooms

available. Facilities include: Restaurant, bar, reading room, gymnasium and steam room. Bicycles available for guests.

LA VALISE
Tonalá 53, Mexico City, 52-55-5286-9560
www.lavalise.mx
NEIGHBORHOOD: Roma
Probably the hottest, hippest place in all Mexico City is Roma, loaded with shops, restaurants and bars, but few hotels. However, there's a great little lodging owned by French ex-patriot designer Emmanuel Picault, who opened a few rooms above his distinctive shop in a building dating back to the 1920s on a street lined with trees. Picault, originally from Normandy, has designed interiors for the local **Chic by Accident** (a trendy shop) and also a local nightclub, **M. N. Roy** (in a subterranean space behind a rundown ice cream parlor, also in Roma), as well as Nüba, one of the

better nightclubs in Paris. The décor in the 3 rooms he offers for rent here are very modern, but reflect his appreciation of Mesoamerican art of the Mayans and Aztecs. There's a hammock strung up in the atrium, adding a whimsical touch. Each of the 3 suites offer different takes on black-and-white, while the outside of the building reflects an ornate Beaux-Arts look. There's no restaurant, but one of the best restaurants in the city is nearby, **Rosetta**, and waiters will come over with breakfast, lunch or dinner if you ask them.

LAS ALCOBAS

Presidente Masaryk 390, Mexico City, +52 55 3300 3900

www.lasalcobas.com

NEIGHBORHOOD: Federal District

Located in one of the most exclusive neighborhoods of Mexico City, his masterfully designed boutique hotel offers 35 guest rooms, suites and penthouses. Most of the residences offer wraparound terraces and all feature state of the art technology. The hotel features in room spa facilities, rain showers, and Jacuzzi. Facilities include on-site restaurant and spa.

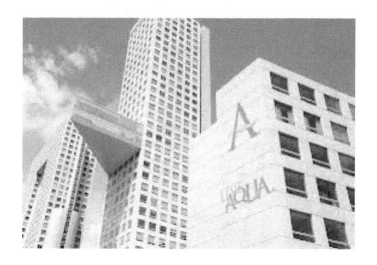

LIVE AQUA BOSQUES

Paseo de Los Tamarindos 98, Mexico City, +52 55
9177 8400

www.liveaqua.com

NEIGHBORHOOD: Bosques de las Lomas

This unique and innovative hotel offers a relaxed
ambiance in a luxury setting. Now, bear in mind that
it's about an hour outside downtown in the Santa Fe
neighborhood, but it attracts a good clientele. The
hotel offers 114 luxurious guest rooms and 23 suites.
Amenities include: 46-inch Smart TV, Nespresso
coffeemaker, and motorized drapes. Every floor has its
own concierge. On-site restaurant and Spa.

RED TREE HOUSE
Culiacan 6, Mexico City, +52 55 5584 3829
www.theredtreehouse.com
NEIGHBORHOOD: Federal District
This is Mexico City's top B&B. You'll get personal
service and lots of hospitality. This is not a luxury
hotel but the rooms are tasteful with beautiful
surroundings. Amenities include: free wireless
Internet and a free breakfast. Conveniently located
near parks, restaurants, art galleries, shopping, and
city transportation.

ST REGIS
Paseo de la Reforma 439, Mexico City, 52 55 5228
1818
www.starwoodhotels.com/stregis/
NEIGHBORHOOD: Cuauhtemoc
Located in the first 15 floors of the sleek, 31-story
Torre Libertad (designed by Cesar Pelli), the St. Regis
Mexico City overlooks the Paseo de la

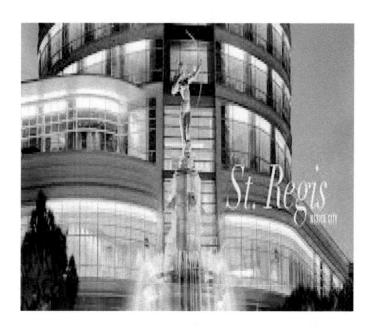

Reforma. The luxury hotel offers 189 large and very plush rooms, including 36 suites and a grand presidential suite. Amenities include: Remede bath amenities, GDA system for master control, oversized flat screen TVs, CD/DVD player, and in-room digital movie system. Wi-Fi Internet Access available. Hotel facilities include: King Cole Bar and a Spa and Fitness Center from which there happens to be one of the best views in the whole city.

**St Regis (center above) and the
King Cole Bar (below)**

Chapter 4
WHERE TO EAT

One good thing about eating in Mexico City is that it's possible to eat cheaply here from one end of town to the other. The street food is really terrific, maybe the best in the world except for certain cities in Southeast Asia. Every corner will have great food on it.

AZUL CONDESA
Nuevo León 68, Cuauhtémoc, Hipódromo, Mexico
City, +52 55 5286 6268
www.azul.rest
CUISINE: Mexican
DRINKS: Full Bar
SERVING: Breakfast, Lunch
PRICE RANGE: $$$
NEIGHBORHOOD: Condesa
Chef Ricardo Munoz Zurita offers a menu of authentic
Mexican cuisine in a simple atmosphere of wooden
tables and chairs. Though the dining room is electric
with activity, try to get one of the tables in the atrium
garden if you can swing it. Very lush and tropical.
Menu favorites include: Beef drizzled in a smoky
Oaxacan mole, Veracruz style fish, and ancient Mayan
dishes. Try the "enigmatico" chichilo negro, which is
one of the 7 Oaxaca moles you seldom see. (It's made
with chihuacle pepper ashes and is usually served
with beef.)

AZUL HISTÓRICO
Isabel la Católica, 30, Centro Historico A, 52 55 5510 1316
www.azul.rest
CUISINE: Mexican
DRINKS: Full Bar
SERVING: Brunch, Lunch, Dinner
PRICE RANGE: $$$
NEIGHBORHOOD: Downtown south / Centro Sur
With lights in the thick-branched trees overhead, you couldn't find a more romantic spot than this popular restaurant serving favorites like Stuffed Duck Fritters dipped in mole and Black Chichilo Chiluacle Chili served with venison. This is also a great place for breakfast, serving favorites like chilaquiles, Mexican eggs, and enchiladas. Try the delicious house-made chocolate cake served with gorgonzola cheese ice cream.

BEATRICITA
Londres 190-D, Mexico City, 52 55 5511 4213
www.beatricita.com
CUISINE: Mexican street food
DRINKS: Beer & Wine
SERVING: Dinner
PRICE RANGE: $
NEIGHBORHOOD: Colonia Zona Rosa
If you're a fan of tacos, this is your place. Here in Coyoacán's main market you'll find a variety of great tacos and daily specials. One of the differences in the carnitas tacos you get in America and what you get here is that here they have cooked a whole pig, and you can choose if you want belly, leg, snout, whatever part of the pig you want. In America, it's usually just dry shredded pork, hardly the same.

BELMONDO
Tabasco 109, Mexico City, +55 62 73 2079
www.belmondo.com.mx/
CUISINE: Deli, Sandwiches
DRINKS: Wines
SERVING: Lunch & Dinner
PRICE RANGE: $
NEIGHBORHOOD: Roma Norte
This eatery draws lots of young creative and trendy
types and offers a simple menu featuring salads,
sandwiches as spot on and good as any you've had
anywhere. Also a curated list of wines by the glass.
Menu favorites include: the French dip with roast
beef and gravy, or the grilled cheese with caramelized
onions. Closed Sundays. Be prepared for a wait.

BÓSFORO
Luis Moya 31, Mexico City, +52 55 5512 1991
No Website
CUISINE: Mexican

DRINKS: Full Bar
SERVING: Breakfast, Lunch, Dinner
PRICE RANGE: $$
NEIGHBORHOOD: Federal District
This small friendly neighborhood bar specializes in mezcales and offers a menu of Mexican bar food with favorites like the quesadilla and tapas. Try the desserts especially if you're a chocolate lover.

CABRERA 7
Calle Plaza Luis Cabrera 7, Miguel Hidalgo, Mexico City, 52 55 5264 4531
CUISINE: Mexican
DRINKS: Full Bar
SERVING: Brunch, Lunch, Dinner
PRICE RANGE: $$
NEIGHBORHOOD: Roma Norte
This superb two-level restaurant and lounge bar

(overlooking the gorgeous fountains decorating **Plaza Luis Cabrera**), and has a menu featuring Mexican cuisine from all regions. Menu favorites include: Oaxacan mole, cochinita pibil, and of course the tacos and tortas. This place makes for great people-watching as artists set up makeshift stalls to sell their wares and the whole population flows by in a continuous and colorful parade of humanity.

CAFÉ EL POPULAR RESTAURANTE
5 de Mayo, No. 50-52, Mexico City, 55 5518-6081
CUISINE: Cafe
DRINKS: No Booze
SERVING: 24 hours
PRICE RANGE: $$
NEIGHBORHOOD: Central Historic District
This 24-hour café offers great Mexican breakfast like huevos rancheros or enchiladas verdes under a wood beamed ceiling. Great coffees and pastries. If you're lucky there will be live music.

CAFÉ NIN
Calle Havre 73, Juárez, Mexico, +52 55 5207 7065
www.cafenin.com.mx
CUISINE: Breakfast
DRINKS: No Booze
SERVING: Breakfast
PRICE RANGE: $$
NEIGHBORHOOD: Juárez
Great choice for breakfast and the most popular brunch spot in the area. Impressive selection of baked goods – everything from doughnuts to croissants and the best-ever guava cheese pastries. Delicious cappuccino. Nice small plates as well, like the avocado & squid ceviche.

CAFÉ PASSMAR

Calle Adolfo Prieto s/n Local 237, Mexico City, +52
55 5669 1994
www.cafepassmar.com
CUISINE: Cafeteria/Coffeehouse
NEIGHBORHOOD: Benito Juárez
Just a coffeehouse that offers a full range of coffees
beyond Starbucks presentation along with fruit
smoothies, herbal teas, and frappes.

CHURRERIA EL MORO

Eje Central Lázaro Cárdenas 42, Col. Centro
Histórico, Ciudad de México, +52 52 551 20896
www.elmoro.mx
CUISINE: Coffee shop
DRINKS: No Booze
SERVING: Open 24 hours
PRICE RANGE: $
NEIGHBORHOOD: Centro Sur
Churros, churros, churros. They have to be eaten
when they're warm to be appreciated. Here at this
bakery, where they do things the old-fashioned way,
they make 'em to order, so you get fresh churros
with a variety of toppings, everything from deep dark
chocolate to dulce de leche.

CONTRAMAR

Calle de Durango 200, Mexico City, +52 55 5514
9217
www.contramar.com.mx
CUISINE: Seafood
DRINKS: Full Bar
SERVING: Lunch, Dinner
PRICE RANGE: $$$

NEIGHBORHOOD: Condesa
This seafood restaurant is considered one of the chicest dining halls in the whole country, and not so much for its food, which is fine, but for the eclectic mix of artists, hipsters and trendy types it attracts. Blue and white color scheme highlights the high-ceilinged room. Best people-watching in the city. Has a great selection of dishes, including Tuna Tostadas, Oysters & pescado a la talla, Crab Cakes, and Spaghetti with Clams.

COOX HANAL
Calle Isabel la Catolica 83, Centro Histórico, Centro, 06090 Ciudad de México, CDMX,
+52 55 5709 3613
www.cooxhanal.com
CUISINE: Mexican
DRINKS: Full bar
SERVING: Lunch & Dinner
PRICE RANGE: $$$
NEIGHBORHOOD: Central Historic District
Popular eatery (since 1953) on the second floor offering authentic Yucatan fare like *poc chuc* (pork grilled after being marinated in orange juice). Other menu picks: Chamorro and Lime soup. Live music. This place was originally opened by boxer Raul Salazar, from Yucatan's capital, Merida.

DELIRIO

Ave. Monterrey 116-b, Mexico City, +52 55 5584 0870

www.delirio.mx

CUISINE: French/Deli

DRINKS: Beer & Wine Only

SERVING: Breakfast, Lunch & Dinner; closed Mon

PRICE RANGE: $$

NEIGHBORHOOD: Roma Norte

Great place to stop if you're looking for non-Mexican fare. Light dishes like focaccia.

DULCE PATRIA
Anatole France 100, Mexico City, 52 55 3300 3999
www.dulcepatriamexico.com
CUISINE: Mexican
DRINKS: Full Bar
SERVING: Breakfast, Lunch
PRICE RANGE: $$$$
NEIGHBORHOOD: Polanco
Chef Martha Ortiz offers a menu of traditional
Mexican cuisine with a modern twist. It's her
innovative approach that has pushed her to the
forefront of the "New Mexican" cuisine that's
exploding all over the country (and abroad). This 90-
seat eatery features two terraces inside the restaurant
giving an outdoor feel. Definitely begin with her
ceviche. But also try her fabulous "sangritas" as a
chaser after you down a shot of tequila.

EL CARDENAL
Palma 23, México, D.F., +52 55 5521 8815
www.restauranteelcardenal.com

CUISINE: Mexican
DRINKS: Full Bar
SERVING: Breakfast, Lunch, & Dinner
PRICE RANGE: $$
NEIGHBORHOOD: Centro Sur
Located in a beautiful old house, this popular eatery serves authentic Mexican fare. Favorites: Quesadillas with guac, and Chicken with nopales. Popular brunch spot. If you're there for one of the best breakfast in town, get the *huevos en caldo de frijol.*

EL FAROLITO
Altata 19, Col. Condesa, México, D.F., +52 55 5273 7297
www.taqueriaselfarolito.com.mx
CUISINE: Tacos
DRINKS: No Booze
SERVING: Lunch & Dinner
PRICE RANGE: $
NEIGHBORHOOD: Condesa
Delicious Mexican fare prepared right in front of you at this decades-old spot with several locations. Try the Faroladas de Bisteck (Pita bread with steak and cheese). Nice selection of fruit juices.

EL HIDALGUENSE
Campeche 155, Mexico City, +52 55 5564 0538
No Website
CUISINE: Mexican
DRINKS: No Booze
SERVING: Open only 7 a.m. – 5 p.m. Fri - Sun
PRICE RANGE: $$
NEIGHBORHOOD: Roma Sur
A locals' favorite, this Mexican eatery offers a great

selection of barbecue, meats, montalayo, and seafood. Authentic Mexican fare.

EL MAYOR
República de Argentina 15, Col. Centro, Mexico City, 52 55 5704 7580
www.restaurantelmayor.com.mx
CUISINE: Mexican
DRINKS: Full Bar
SERVING: Brunch, Lunch
PRICE RANGE: $$
NEIGHBORHOOD: Centro Histórico
Located on the top floor above a bookstore, this modern restaurant offers a menu of Mexican favorites and European-influenced fusion dishes. This is also a great place for brunch. There's a rooftop bar that overlooks the ruins of the Aztec city.

EL TURIX

Emilio Castelar, 212, Mexico City, 52 55 5280 6449
CUISINE: Mexican
DRINKS: Beer & Wine
SERVING: Lunch, Dinner
PRICE RANGE: $
NEIGHBORHOOD: Colonia Polanco
Located in a dingy storefront, but the food is worth
the visit. There's an outdoor patio and a couple tables
inside. Menu favorites include Cochinita pibil (pork
slowly cooked with achiote that is a specialty of the
Yucatán) and Tamales.

EL VENADITO

Universidad 1701, Col. Chimalistac, México, D.F.,
+52 55 5661 9786
No Web Site
CUISINE: Tacos
DRINKS: Beer &Wine
SERVING: Lunch & Dinner
PRICE RANGE: $
NEIGHBORHOOD: Florida
For over 50 years this place has served typical
Mexican fare to lines of happy customers. Known for
their great Carnitas. Favorites: Enchiladas, tacos al
pastor and French toast dessert. Across the street you
can see the Chapel of San Jose del Atillo.

ENO

Francisco Petrarca 258, Mexico City, +52 55 5531
8535
www.eno.com.mx
CUISINE: Sandwiches
DRINKS: Beer & Wine Only

SERVING: Breakfast, Lunch & Dinner
PRICE RANGE: $$
NEIGHBORHOOD: Polanco
Casual eatery that specializes in sandwiches. Great
spot for breakfast or lunch. Seating is communal.
Favorites include the carnitas de atun (seared tuna)
sandwich.

FLOR DE LIS
Avenida Mazatlan 30, Condesa, Mexico City, 52 55
5211 0060
www.tamalesyatole.com
CUISINE: Mexican
DRINKS: Beer & Wine
SERVING: Dinner
PRICE RANGE: $
NEIGHBORHOOD: Condesa
If you're looking for tamales, this is your place.
There's a nice variety including chicken, peppers,
beef, mole, and sweet (fruit). The atmosphere is
quaint but the food is solid. Menu favorites included
the Chicken and tomato tamale wrapped in banana
leaf.

FONDA MARGARITA
Adolfo Prieto 1364, Mexico City, +52 55 5559 6358
CUISINE: Mexican
DRINKS: No Booze
SERVING: Breakfast, Lunch & Dinner
PRICE RANGE: $
NEIGHBORHOOD: Benito Juarez
Authentic Mexican cuisine typical of the region. Try
the chicharrones in green sauce served with fresh
tortillas and eggs and beans. Very few vegetarian
options. Spanish speaking only.

FONDA MAYORA
Campeche 322, Hipódromo, Mexico City, +52 55
6843 0595
www.fondamayora.com
CUISINE: Mexican
DRINKS: Full bar
SERVING: Breakfast, Lunch & Dinner (early)

PRICE RANGE: $$$
NEIGHBORHOOD: Condesa
Chef Gerardo Vázquez Lugo offers a menu of traditional Mexican fare. The best was the guacamole served from a cart and mixed to order with your choice of onions, tomatoes, and avocado. Everything is served fresh. Not a tourist destination.

HAVRE 77
Havre 77, Col. Juárez, México, D.F., 5208 1070
No Website
CUISINE: French-Mexican
DRINKS: No Booze
SERVING: Breakfast, Lunch; closed Mon & Tues
PRICE RANGE: $$$$
NEIGHBORHOOD: Juárez
Small eatery reminiscent of cafes in Paris. A perfect place to stop when you want a break from Mexican food. Favorites: Steak frites, Escargots du Jour and Laitue (salad with fresh tarragon). Delicious French pastries make this a nice stop early in the morning.

HOSTERIA DE SANTO DOMINGO
Calle Belisario Dominguez 72, 06010 México, D.F., +52 55 5526 5276
No Website
CUISINE: Mexican
DRINKS: Full bar
SERVING: Breakfast, Lunch & Dinner
PRICE RANGE: $$
NEIGHBORHOOD: Centro Norte
Traditional authentic Mexican fare in the city's oldest restaurant that opened in the 1860s. Gourmet dishes featuring meats and fish, like the *chile en nogado*,

large poblano chile peppers stuffed full of ground meat, dried fruit and topped with a rich, creamy sauce. Live music. The atmosphere may remind you of your grandmother's house, or, come to think of it, your great-grandmother's house.

GUZINA OAXACA
Masaryk 513, Mexico City, **+52 55 5282 1820**
www.guzinaoaxaca.com
CUISINE: Mexican
DRINKS: Full bar
SERVING: Breakfast, Lunch & Dinner
PRICE RANGE: $$
NEIGHBORHOOD: Polanco
Chef Alejandro Ruíz recently opened this location of his acclaimed Oaxaca eatery serving contemporary Mexican fare. Here you'll get delicious homemade tortillas, tableside served Oaxacan salsa, and mole. Great choice for breakfast. Make reservations for this place.

LA CASA DE LAS SIRENAS

AV Revolucion 1309 esq Corregidora, Mexico City, 52 55 5593 4916

www.tortaslacastellana.com

CUISINE: Continental

DRINKS: Full Bar

SERVING: Breakfast, Lunch, Dinner

PRICE RANGE: $$$

NEIGHBORHOOD: Centro Histórico (Central Historic)

This charming restaurant overlooks the Cathedral of Mexico City and the National Palace. Menu favorites include: Roast chicken and Rib Eye. Delicious desserts. The restaurant features a tequila salon with dozens of agave spirits and a rooftop with tables that look into the cathedral's garden.

LA CASTELLANA

AV Revolucion 1309 esq Corregidora, Mexico City, 52 55 5593 5767

www.grupocastellano.com.mx

CUISINE: Mexican

DRINKS: Beer & Wine

SERVING: Lunch, Dinner

PRICE RANGE: $

Specializing in tortas, this is just one of five locations. The tortas are made with crisp-crusted and light bread, pickled jalapenos and a variety of fillings. And cheap, cheap, cheap.

LA BARRACA VALENCIANA

Centenario 91-C, Col. Del Carmen, Mexico City, +52
55 5658 1880
www.labarracavalenciana.com
CUISINE: Spanish/Tapas/Small Plates
DRINKS: Beer & Wine Only
SERVING: Lunch & Dinner; closed Sun
PRICE RANGE: $$
NEIGHBORHOOD: Coyoacán
Small eatery (only 12 tables) serving a menu of tapas
and small plates. Favorites include: Squid Roman,
Grilled chicken breast and Chamorro veal. Specials
change weekly.

LA DOCENA OYSTER BAR

Av. Álvaro Obregón 31, Mexico City, +52 55 5208
0833
www.ladocena.com.mx
CUISINE: Seafood
DRINKS: Full bar
SERVING: Lunch & Dinner
PRICE RANGE: $$$
NEIGHBORHOOD: Roma Norte
Seafood eatery specializing in oysters and barbecue.
Favorite dish: Baby squid with garlic. Creative
selection of desserts. Reservations recommended.
English menu available.

LALO!

Calle Zacatecas 173, Mexico City, +52 55 5564 3388
www.eat-lalo.com
CUISINE: Breakfast/Pizza
DRINKS: Beer & Wine Only
SERVING: Breakfast, Lunch & Dinner; Lunch only
on Mon
PRICE RANGE: $$
NEIGHBORHOOD: Roma Norte
Chef Eduardo Garcia's casual eatery just across the
street from his more upscale eatery Maximo Bistrot.
Great choice for breakfast – have the French toast.
Amazing selection of pastries and house-made yogurt.
Dinner choices include dishes like freshly made
octopus with arugula.

LARDO

Agustín Melgar 6, Cuauhtemoc, Mexico City, +52 55
5211 7731
www.lardo.mx
CUISINE: French
DRINKS: Full bar
SERVING: Lunch & Dinner
PRICE RANGE: $$
NEIGHBORHOOD: Condesa
Hip eatery with a menu of Mexican and international
cuisine. Great selection of seafood and seasonal
dishes. They will even make dishes to order. Nice
selection of wines.

LAS CAZUELAS DE LA ABUELA

Av San Jeronimo 630, Mexico City, +52 55 5683
8720
https://las-cazuelas-de-la-abuela.business.site
CUISINE: Mexican
DRINKS: Full Bar
SERVING: Dinner
PRICE RANGE: $
NEIGHBORHOOD: Pedregal
This family restaurant offers a menu of Mexican
cuisine with Poblano overtones. The menu features 25
different stews and delicious peneques – a deep-fried
quesadilla with green and red pumpkin-seed sauce.

LOS PANCHOS

Calle Tolstoi 9, Miguel Hidalgo, +52 55 5254 5390
www.lospanchos.mx
CUISINE: Mexican
DRINKS: Full bar
SERVING: Breakfast, Lunch & Dinner

PRICE RANGE: $$
NEIGHBORHOOD: Anzures
Great place for a family dinner.
Traditional Mexican eatery that's worth a try. Great dishes and the steak here is exceptional (not your typical American steak). Nice selection of desserts.

MAISON ARTEMISIA
Tonalá 23, Cuauhtémoc, Mexico City, +52 55 6303 2471
www.maisonartemisia.com
CUISINE: French
DRINKS: Full bar
SERVING: Lunch & Dinner; closed Sun
PRICE RANGE: $$$
NEIGHBORHOOD: Roma Norte
Upscale dining with an upstairs piano bar. Restaurant offers a nice selection of seafood and beef. Favorites include: Grilled octopus and Short-rib ravioli.
This place is famous for its imported absinthe and absinthe-based cocktails.

MAXIMO BISTROT LOCAL
Tonalá 133, Mexico City, 52 55 5264 4291
www.maximobistrot.com.mx
CUISINE: Mexican, Italian, French
DRINKS: Wine
SERVING: Lunch, Dinner
PRICE RANGE: $$$$
NEIGHBORHOOD: Roma Norte
This rustic bistro, run by a young husband-and-wife team, offers a daily menu featuring ingredients found in the local markets. It has an open kitchen and has handwritten daily menus. Menu favorites include:

Lamb loin and Tartar of Steelhead. Reservations required.

MERCADO ROMA COYOACAN

Miguel Angel Quevedo 353, Mexicto DF, 55 2155 9435

www.mrc.mercadoroma.com

NEIGHBORHOOD: Coyoacán

Over 40 wildly diverse vendors occupy the 3 floors of this spectacular market, and a lot of them are eateries offering up authentic Mexican fare. While this is basically a collection of upscale food vendors that replicate the down-and-dirty street food you can find all over the city, in this place things are a little tidier, and the excitement stems from the fact that you can sample Mexican-fusion this or that, getting tastes from the far corners of this country. You can get tacos from 9 different regions of the country. But also elements of cuisine from around the world, all blended into Mexicsn cuisince. An Italian vendor serves tacos, but the taco is *piadina*, which is like a tortilla, but comes from Italy. Hundreds of surprising (and pleasing) combinations like this will enchant you. If you're on a short visit, this place ought to be a must, because you'll get to experience so much so fast.

MERENDERO LAS LUPITAS

Plaza Santa Catarina 4, Col. Del Carmen, México, D.F., +52 55 5554 3353

www.merenderolaslupitas.com.mx/

CUISINE: Mexican

DRINKS: No Booze

SERVING: Breakfast, Lunch; closed Mon & Tues

PRICE RANGE: $$

NEIGHBORHOOD: Coyoacán
Family-run eatery offering authentic Northern
Mexican fare. Try the atole (a corn based drink served
hot). Favorites: Chimichangas, egg & bean dishes and
Flan.

MERO TORO
Calle Amsterdam 204, Mexico City, +52 55 5564
7799
www.merotoro.mx
CUISINE: Northern Mexican
DRINKS: Full Bar
SERVING: Dinner
PRICE RANGE: $$$
NEIGHBORHOOD: Condesa
Open since 2010, this eatery brings the surf-and-
turf cuisine of Baja California to the Mexican
highlands. Chef Jair Tellez created the expansive
menu. Selections start with the small plate men

featuring dishes like Ceviche ligero but don't forget the delicious main courses like Gently roasted grouper served on a bed of puréed cauliflower.

MOG
Frontera 168, Col. Roma, 52 55 5264 1629
CUISINE: Asian
DRINKS: Beer & Wine Only
SERVING: Lunch, Dinner
PRICE RANGE: $$
NEIGHBORHOOD: Roma Norte
This popular eatery offers a menu of sushi, Japanese style dishes and fusion. The bar serves a variety of Mexican and Japanese beers and sakes. Menu favorites include: Sushi rolls, Teriyaki Chicken and Yakimeshi. Desserts favorites include the green tea cake.

PAPRIKA
Masella 61, Col. Juarez, Mexico City, +52 55 5533 0303
CUISINE: Mediterranean/Moroccan/Arabian
DRINKS: Full bar
SERVING: Lunch & Dinner; closed Sun
PRICE RANGE: $$
NEIGHBORHOOD: Juárez
Middle eastern eatery with a menu of small plate dishes created by Chef Josefina Santacruz. Popular dishes like Lamb and lentils served with rice, pistachios and apricots. Nice menu of teas.

PASTELERIA LA GRAN VIA
Amsterdan 288-A, Mexico City, +52 55 5574 4008
www.pastelerialagranvia.com

CUISINE: Bakery/Specialty Grocery
NEIGHBORHOOD: Condesa
Popular bakery featuring a variety of breads, pastries, doughnuts, cakes and cookies. Great meringues and low-sugar options.

PUJOL
Tennyson 133, Mexico City, 52 55 5545 4111
www.pujol.com.mx
CUISINE: Mexican/Fusion
DRINKS: Full Bar
SERVING: Brunch, Lunch, Dinner
PRICE RANGE: $$$$
NEIGHBORHOOD: Polanco
With a reputation as one of the world's best restaurants (and hardest to get into with only a baker's dozen tables), this Mexican eatery mixes modern (mostly French-inspired) and ancient culinary techniques. Prix-fix menu. Menu favorites include: Fish ceviche taco and Fried pork belly. As an example of Chef Enrique Olvera's innovative culinary talents,

I ordered tacos that had baby lamb, avocado-pera purée and the pungently aromatic herb, *hoja santa*. Delicious. This is why Olvera is Mexico's most famous chef.

QUINTONIL
Newton 55, Mexico City, 52 55 5280 1660
www.quintonil.com
CUISINE: Mexican
DRINKS: Full Bar
SERVING: Dinner
PRICE RANGE: $$$
NEIGHBORHOOD: Polanaco
This place takes traditional Mexican cuisine to the next level. Great margaritas and Mexican wines. Menu favorites include: Swiss chard tamale with raison puree; delicate slices of *chilacayote* squash and charred tortillas are topped with mole; *Huauzontle*, which is something similar to broccoli, is fried and served with salsa and cheese from Chiapas.

RESTAURANTE BAR CHON
Regina 160, 06090 México, D.F. +52 55 5542 0873
CUISINE: Mexican; Pre-Hispanic cuisine as well
DRINKS: Full bar
SERVING: Lunch & Dinner; closed Sunday
PRICE RANGE: $$$
NEIGHBORHOOD: Centro Sur
Traditional Mexican fare with most entrees based around the tortilla, rice and beans. This is one of the few places that also serves Pre-Hispanic food, so you can see what it was like to eat before Europeans arrived to muck it all up for the Indians. Unique offerings featuring insects, grasshoppers, worms,

ant larvae and wild boar. Try the *pulque* ("blood of the gods"), a flavored beverage. A once-in-a-lifetime experience.

RESTAURANTE NICOS
Av. Cuitlahuac 3102, Mexico City, +52 55 5396 7090
www.nicosmexico.mx
WEBSITE DOWN AT PRESSTIME
CUISINE: Mexican
DRINKS: Full bar
SERVING: Breakfast, Lunch & Dinner; closed Sun
PRICE RANGE: $$$
NEIGHBORHOOD: Clavería
Not your typical Mexican eatery, great menu of "Nouvelle Mexican cuisine." Imaginative dishes and what many say is the "best" guacamole in the world. If you have a taste for sweets try the chocolate mousse cake. Menu in Spanish but the waiters do a good job of describing the dishes.
Good choice for breakfast.

ROKAI
Rio Ebro 87, Mexico City, 55 5207 7543
http://edokobayashi.com/index.php/rokai/
CUISINE: Japanese
DRINKS: Beer, Wine & Sake
SERVING: Lunch, Dinner; closed Sunday
PRICE RANGE: $
NEIGHBORHOOD: Cuauhtémoc
A favorite among locals and foodies, this small Japanese eatery serves up famous dishes like Rokai, mussels sake, tuna, rib eye and duck, red snapper with Himalayan salt and yuzu paste and Ensenada Octopus sashimi. They also have a menu with nine

or ten courses –changing daily. They also have a
real standout menu item in their fried chicken. What
makes it different (and a delightful surprise for a
South Carolina boy like myself) is that it's marinated
in sake. The bar offers hot sake, green tea, Sapporo
beer and wine.

SUD777
Blvd. de la Luz 777, Col. Jardines del Pedregal,
México, D.F., +52 55 5568 4777
www.sud777.com.mx/web2
CUISINE: Mexican
DRINKS: Full Bar
SERVING: Breakfast, Lunch, & Dinner
PRICE RANGE: $$$
NEIGHBORHOOD: Jardines del Pedregal
Great dining experience in a classic restaurant open
since 2008 that offers cutting edge innovative cuisine
while relying on traditional Mexican ingredients.
Updated, modern, but still somehow traditional. The
crisscrossing beams above give the place a modern
look, as vines weave in and out of nooks and crannies.
Light brown wooden tables mix with the blacks and
grays to highlight the intimate décor. The chef swears
he never uses any produce that's not Mexican. (I
believe him.) There is a tasting menu, which I highly
recommend. Be sure to get the wine pairing, because
this place has one of the best selections of really local
Mexican wines to be had in the city. Too many other
upscale restaurants focus on foreign labels. Favorites:
Tuna tostada with soy, Lechon pork, poblano chiles,
Cotija cheese, a foie gras that's made locally and Crab
ceviche. (There also a super good sushi bar, **Kokeshi**,
tucked away inside this place.)

TABERNA DEL LEON

Altamirano 46, Col.Tizapán San Ángel, 01000
México, D.F., +52 55 5616 2110
CUISINE: Mexican gourmet
DRINKS: Full bar
SERVING: Lunch & Dinner
PRICE RANGE: $$$$
NEIGHBORHOOD: San Angel

Beautiful upscale though casual eatery offering an
exceptional dining experience. Favorites: Pork chop
with Brussel sprouts and Foie gras; *robalo a los tres
chiles* (bass cooked with a three-pepper chili sauce).
Excellent desserts like Chocolate cake served with
raspberry ice cream.

TACOS DON JUAN

Atlixco 42, 06760 México, D.F., +52 55 5286 0816
No Website
CUISINE: Tacos
DRINKS: No Booze
SERVING: Lunch only
PRICE RANGE: $
NEIGHBORHOOD: La Condesa

Authentic hole-in-the-wall joint offering a rotating
menu of fresh tacos. On Sunday, for instance, they'll
serve tacos with *bistec con longaniza* (beef with
sausage meat) topped off with a dollop of beans; on
Friday or Saturday, you'll get *carnitas* (deep-fried
pork). It doesn't matter what day you go, though,
because every day the tacos are great, which accounts
for the lines and why they've been here for so many
years. Order at the counter – no inside seating, just
outside.

TACOS MANOLO
Luz Saviñón 1305 (bet. Anaxágoras and Cauhtémoc), Mexico City, 52 55 4437 1463
No Website
CUISINE: Mexican
DRINKS:
SERVING: Lunch, Dinner
PRICE RANGE: $$
NEIGHBORHOOD: Colonia Del Valle
This busy stand is all about tacos. Try the classic Manolo, chopped bistec with onion and bacon.

TAQUERIA EL CALIFA
Altata 22, Mexico City, +52 55 5271 7666
www.elcalifa.com.mx/web/
CUISINE: Mexican
DRINKS: Beer & Wine
SERVING: Dinner
PRICE RANGE: $$
NEIGHBORHOOD: Condesa
A popular taqueria with traditional favorites like the chicharon de queso and the Gaona conqueso.

TAQUERIA EL PROGRESO

Calle Maestro Antonio Caso 30, Col. Tabacalera, +52 55 5546 4700

https://taqueriaelprogreso.negocio.site/

CUISINE: Tacos

DRINKS: No Booze

SERVING: Breakfast, Lunch; closed Mon & Tues

PRICE RANGE: $

NEIGHBORHOOD: Tabacalera

Tacos at this great little sidewalk café are served with a variety of meats and lots of toppings including mashed potatoes, beans, cactus, manzanita peppers and onions. Cow head tacos served here (tacos de cabeza), as well as the excellent cow brain. (Check out the juice bar next door.)

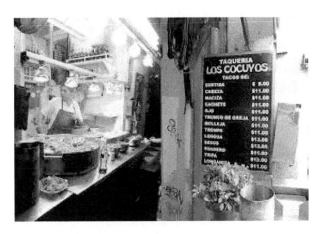

TAQUERIA LOS COCUYOS

Calle Bolívar 56, Mexico City, 52 55 5518 4231

No Website

CUISINE: Tacos

DRINKS: Full Bar

SERVING: Lunch, Dinner

PRICE RANGE: $
NEIGHBORHOOD: Centro
This little taqueria offers up an interesting menu of tacos. Menu favorites include: Suadero (braised and seared beef) and Beef tongue taco.

TETETLAN

Av. de Las Fuentes 180, Col. Jardines del Pedregal, Ciudad de México, +52 55 5668 5335
www.tetetlan.com
CUISINE: Mexican
DRINKS: Full Bar
SERVING: Breakfast, Lunch, & Dinner
PRICE RANGE: $$
NEIGHBORHOOD: Pedregal
Located off the beaten path is this ultra-trendy eatery, that uses many different kinds of stone in its walls, rocks, bricks, poured concrete. Lots of weird angles, nooks and crannies. Completely charming. The name of this place actually means "place of many stones." You'll love it. They offer a menu of international and regional cuisine, boasting that over 90% of what they use comes from Mexico. Favorites: Roasted huitlacoche (this is a fungus that grows on corn), dried crickets with lemon and Tamales with hoja santa. Nice selection of tequilas.

TORTAS EL CAPRICHO
Augusto Rodin, 407, Mexico City, 52 55 3330 3935
CUISINE: Mexican
DRINKS: Beer & Wine
SERVING: Lunch, Dinner
PRICE RANGE: $
NEIGHBORHOOD: Colonia Mixoac
This eatery, very popular among the locals, specializes
in tortas, large cake sandwiches, and offers nearly 50
varieties.

YUBAN
Colima 268, Mexico City, 52 55 6387 0358
www.yuban.mx
CUISINE: Mexican
DRINKS: Full Bar
SERVING: Lunch, Dinner

PRICE RANGE: $

NEIGHBORHOOD: Roma Norte

Chef Paloma Ortiz offers a menu featuring a variety of traditional recipes with a contemporary flair. There's a big emphasis on the *moles* from Oaxaca Sierre Norte region. Menu favorites include: Smoky chichilo and the classic tlayuda. Desserts include a multi-dimensional multi-layer chocolate cake made with Oaxacan chocolate. At night the place becomes a hip hangout.

Chapter 5
NIGHTLIFE

BALTRA
Iztaccíhuatl 36D, Cuauhtemoc, Mexico City, +52 55 5264 1279
www.baltra.bar
NEIGHBORHOOD: Condesa
Casual bar that offers a unique selection of cocktails –
many created with tea leaves as one of the ingredients.
Great selection of liquors.
Great comfortable bar with unique cocktails,
knowledgeable bartenders and good design!

EL DEPÓSITO
Álvaro Obregón 21, Local 1, Mexico City, 52-55-5207-8152
www.eldeposito.com.mx
NEIGHBORHOOD: Condesa
This is part of a small chain of beer-bar-bottle shops that offer a wide selection of over 160 beers. Here you'll find a great selection of beer on tap, Mexican micros, European imports, German beers and a few Belgians. There's a terrace, TV, and free popcorn.

EL UNDER
Monterey 80, Col. Roma, 52 55 5511 5475
http://theunder.org/real/
NEIGHBORHOOD: Condesa
Another happening dance club.

FIFTY MILS
Paseo de la Reforma 500, Col. Juárez, México, D.F., +52 55 5230 1806
www.fiftymils.com

NEIGHBORHOOD: Juárez
Amazing quaint bar located in the **Four Seasons Hotel**. The Manhattan is their signature cocktail and it's top-notch. The bartenders are pros. But look closely at the "Creations" cocktail menu, which has cocktails unique to this wonderful lounge. Like Ant Man, which uses mescal, ants, egg whites, avocado, hoja santa bitters, soda water & lemongrass syrup. And that's just one cocktail! Plenty more to keep you busy. Hungry? Try the bar snacks like Grilled octopus with pineapple. Since you're here at the Four Seasons, try out the main restaurant, **IL BECCO**, featuring superior cuisine from the Piedmont region and a wondrous Italian wine list that will raise an eyebrow or two.

LA HERMOSA HORTENSIA
Callejón de la Amargura 4, Plaza Garibaldi 4, 52-55-5529-7316
No Website
NEIGHBORHOOD: Centro Norte
Located on the far corner of the Plaza Garibaldi, this

pulquería is a must-stop for visitors. It's a 77-year old pulque bar that serves the lightly alcoholic Aztec drink, made from the maguey plant. The drink has the color of milk and comes in flavors like strawberry and coconut. This bar is included in the Museos Vivos project (which highlights "Living Museums"- every day venues that have cultural and historic significance).

LA NACIONAL
Orizaba 161, Mexico City, +52 55 5264 3106
No Website
NEIGHBORHOOD: Roma Norte
More of a bar than a restaurant with a very long list of Mexican microbrews. Great local hangout.

LICORERIA LIMANTOUR
Alvaro Obregon 106, Mexico City, +52 55 5264 4122
www.limantour.tv
NEIGHBORHOOD: Roma Norte
Popular bar that has been awarded the title as being "one of the best 50 bars in the world." Impressive cocktail list. Menu of bar snacks available – fries served with 4 different sauces.

M.N. ROY
Mérida 186, San Luis Potosi
NEIGHBORHGOOD: Roma
www.mnroyclub.com

Emmanuel Picault opened this club and named it after the Indian revolutionary and founder of the Communist parties in both Mexico and India. It's super cool and gorgeously designed. Had throbbing house music late into the night. Dress to impress. It's a slick crowd here, even though the outside is designed to look like a simple ice cream parlor with a door the color of pink carnations.

PATRICK MILLER
Mérida 17, Mexico City, 52 55 5511 5406
www.patrickmiller.com.mx
WEBSITE DOWN AT PRESSTIME
NEIGHBORHOOD: Roma Norte
This is an old school disco featuring high-energy '80s
dance music, laser lights and neon graffiti. Named
after a popular DJ, this club opened during the Gloria
Gayner golden days of disco and has been running
strong ever since. The eclectic crowd is filled with
flashy dressers, flamboyant transvestites, and disco
divas. No hard liquor here, just beer.

PULQUERIA LOS INSURGENTES

Ave. de los Insurgentes Sur 226, Mexico City, +52 55 2767 5227
No Website
NEIGHBORHOOD: Roma Norte
Typical dive bar with loud music and sawdust on the floor. Multi-level bar including a dance floor. Menu of bar snacks. Live music and DJs on weekends. They serve flavored pulque -blended fresh juice mixed with tequila.

RHODESIA CLUB SOCIAL

Durango, 181, 52 55 5533 8208
www.clubsocialrhodesia.tv
NEIGHBORHGOOD: Roma

Chapter 6
WHAT TO SEE & DO

ANAHUACALLI MUSEUM
Museo 150, San Pablo Tepetlapa, Mexico City, +52
55 5617 3797
www.museoanahuacalli.org.mx
NEIGHBORHOOD: Coyoacán
Designed by Diego Rivera, this museum houses the
artist's quirky collection of over 60,000 pre-Hispanic
pieces. The museum is built out of black volcanic
stone and resembles a pyramid. The collection
includes funerary urns, masks, and sculptures from
the ancient culture of Teotihuacan. Minimal admission
fee.

ANTIGUO COLEGIO DE SAN ILDEFONSO

Justo Sierra 16, Mexico City, +52 55 3602 0035

www.sanildefonso.org.mx

NEIGHOBORHOOD: Centro Norte

This 18th-century former Jesuit school reopened as a museum and cultural center in 1992. The museum features permanent and temporary art and archeological exhibitions. Many come to view the many murals painted on the walls by artists like José Clemente Orozco, Fernando Leal, and Diego Rivera (who also has a lot of works on display at the **Palacio Nacional** a few blocks away). A gift shop is located in the patio of the Colegio Grande offering a selection of museum publications, handcrafted jewelry, ceramics and textiles.

CASA MUSEO LUIS BARRAGAN

General Francisco Ramirez 12, Mexico City, +52 55 5515 4908

www.casaluisbarragan.org

NEIGHBORHOOD: Daniel Garza

This is the former home of the great Mexican Modernist Luis Barragán. The museum is a must-see for lovers of architecture and exhibits Barragán's work. It's often used by visiting architects. Modest entrance fee.

CASTILLO DE CHAPULTEPEC

Bosque de Chapultepec, Mexico City, 52 55 4040 5215

www.mnh.inah.gob.mx

WEBSITE DOWN AT PRESSTIME

NEIGHBORHOOD: Federal District

ADMISSION: Nominal fee, free on Sundays

Located on top of Chapultepec Hill, this is the only Royal Castle in North America. It was used to house the Mexican Emperor Maximilian I. This site was a

sacred place for Aztecs and the buildings were used as a Military Academy, an Imperial residence, a Presidential home and observatory. Today the hilltop castle houses the **Museo Nacional de Historia (National History Museum)**, with marble terraces, fountains and historic artifacts. You can climb up on foot (I did it one, but never again). It's worth the trip for the views alone. But the fountains, the marble floors and the historical exhibits make it even more special. Manet made a famous painting Maximilian's execution, and you can see how it was influenced by Goya's painting "The Third of May 1808" depicting the execution of Spanish soldiers resisting Napoleon's invasion of Spain in the Peninsular War.

CENTRO CULTURAL UNIVERSITARIO
(University Cultural Center)
Avenida Insurgentes Sur 3000, Mexico City, 52 55
5622 7185
www.cultura.unam.mx
Located in a woodsy section of the university campus,
this center is comprised of five theaters, including
the Sala Nezahualcóyotl, home of the UNAM
Philharmonic; the Teatro Alarcón, a drama stage; and
the Sala Miguel Covarrubias, a contemporary dance
venue. The cinema here shows Mexican and European
films.

DAVID POMPA
Colima 264, Mexico City, +52 55 6583 5027
www.davidpompa.com
NEIGHBORHOOD: Roma Norte
Design studio of David Pompa selling high-end
lighting and furniture. A favorite among designers.

EAT MEXICO CULINARY TOURS

Sinaloa 149, Mexico City, +52 1 55 3504 2135

www.eat-mexico.com

NEIGHBORHOOD: Roma

Small private culinary tours of Mexico City. Get a taste of what the locals eat. This tour takes you through the streets of Central Mexico where you'll sample street food, tacos and visit select markets. You'll also get a history of the food you're eating. Tours led by local, bilingual guides who share local history and culinary tips. Six routes to choose from. Tours are approximately 4 hours long.

ELENA GARRO CULTURAL CENTER

Calle Fernández Leal No. 43, Mexico City, +52 55 3003 4081

www.educal.com.mx/elenagarro/

NEIGHBORHOOD: Coyoacán,

Beautiful cultural center designed my Mexican architects Fernanda Canales and Arquitectura 911sc. An old house has been transformed into a modern looking cultural center with a library and series of gardens and courtyards.

GOODBYE FOLK

Colima 198, Cuauhtémoc, Mexico City, +52 55 5525 4109

www.goodbyefolk.com

NEIGHBORHOOD: Roma

Unique boutique that offers fashions and custom made shoes with an onsite hair salon.

Boutique. hairdresser, shoes made to order, free to all Mexico. Boutique, hair salon, custom made shoes.

-we ship all around the world. Fashions like jackets, sweaters, and shirts all have a vintage feel.

HILARIO GALGUERA
Francisco Pimentel 3, Mexico City, 52 55 5546 9001
www.galeriahilariogalguera.com/nueva
NEIGHBORHOOD: San Rafael
Perfect place to catch up top-notch contemporary Mexican artists' work, like Bosco Sodi and Daniel Lezama. Also exhibits international artists like Damien Hirst.

JARDÍN BOTÁNICO (Park)
Tercer Circuito exterior; Ciudad Universitaria, Mexico City, 52 55 5622 9047
www.ibiologia.unam.mx/jardin/
ADMISSSION: Free
NEIGHBORHOOD: University City
This park and garden highlights Mexico's plant diversity. The park is divided into 4 sections that reflect the country's different climate zones. One of the highlights of the park is a greenhouse filled with rare orchids, but as you stroll through the trails, you'll encounter volcanic rocks and see examples of cactuses and succulents that are endangered species. Closed on Mondays.

JUMEX MUSEUM
MUSEO JUMEX
Miguel de Cervantes Saavedra 303, 52 55 5395 2618
NEIGHBORHOOD: Granada
www.fundacionjumex.org
David Chipperfield designed the Jumex, which focuses on contemporary artwork. Opened November

2013. When I first saw this collection, it was called the Coleccion Jumex and was on view in an old juice factory a bit out of town where it was Latin America's largest privately held art collection. Think Cy Twombly, Pedro Reynes, etc. The whole thing makes a much better impression in the Chipperfield building, needless to say.

KURIMANZUTTO GALLERY
Gob. Rafael Rebollar 94, Col. San Miguel Chapultepec, 52-55-5256-2408
www.kurimanzutto.com/en/
Though this gallery is known for representing the top Mexican artists working today, it also has an impressive roster of international artists. Gabriel Orozco, Damian Ortega, Daniel Guzman and Dr Lakra all exhibit their work here, as well as Rirkrit Tiravanija and Jimmie Durham, just to name a few of the more prominent names.

MERCADO DE XOCHIMILCO
Nuevo Leon, Colonia Xochimilco
Farmer's Market OPEN DAILY
NEIGHBORHOOD: Xochimilco
This open-air Farmer's Market offers great shopping opportunities for farm-fresh produce and other items like the city's best barbacoa de borrego (slow-cooked lamb). The market is also a unique dining option with a variety of Mexican dishes including barbeque, quesadillas, tacos, stew, and pambazos.

METROPOLITAN CATHEDRAL

Plaza de la Constitución, Mexico City, 52 55 5510
0440

No Website

NEIGHBORHOOD: Central Historic District

Opened in 1813, this is one of the oldest and largest
Roman Catholic cathedrals in the Americas. This
cathedral also acts as the seat of the Roman Catholic
Archdiocese of Mexico. You can go to the roof of this
cathedral where the view is spectacular as it overlooks
what's left of the ruins (in the Templo Mayor) of
the Aztec city that once existed here. (That city was
called Tenochtitlán—try saying that fast 5 times.)
There's a bar and restaurant up here called **El Mayor**,
so you can get a cool drink after the long climb up.

MUSEO CASA DE LEON TROTSKY

Ave. Rio Churubusco 410, Mexico City, +52 55 5658 8732

www.museocasadeleontrotsky.blogspot.com

NEIGHBORHOOD: Coyoacán

ADMISSION: Moderate fee

The house where exiled Russian leader Leon Trotsky spent his final days has been transformed into a museum. Looking more like a fortress than a home complete with turrets for armed guards, this site is the final resting place for one of the most important figures of the Russian Revolution.

All information in Spanish only. English guides available for groups of five or more with reservations.

MUSEO CASA DEL RISCO

Plaza de San Jacinto 15, Mexico City, +52 55 5616 2711

www.museocasadelrisco.org

NEIGHBORHOOD: San Ángel

ADMISSION: Free

Founded in 1958, this Cultural Center exhibits Mexican and European painting, sculpture, applied arts, textile works, and art objects purchased by politician Don Isidro Fabela. Revolving exhibitions along with the permanent collection, a library and a gift shop.

MUSEO DEL JUGUETE ANTIGUO MÉXICO

Dr. Olvera 15, Mexico City, 52 55 5558 2100

www.museodeljuguete.mx

NEIGHBORHOOD: Doctores

This multistory museum and art space built originally to house the collection of Roberto Shimizu. The collection mainly consists of mass-produced toys like Mexican action figures, German-made racecars, dolls heads, game pieces and lucha libre wrestlers. Roberto starting his collection in 1955 when he hoarded all his toys. His son now runs this collection of 45,000 items in a place next door to an auto-body shop just south of downtown.

MUSEO DIEGO RIVERA ANAHUACALLI

Calle Museo 150, Mexico City, +52 55 5617 4310

www.museoanahuacalli.org.mx/en/

ADMISSION: Moderate fee

HOURS:11 a.m. – 5:30 p.m. Wed-Sun

Designed by Diego Rivera himself, this impressive

museum made of volcanic stone houses his collection
of pre-Columbian art. The collection includes nearly
50,000 pre-Hispanic art pieces. The second floor
features an exhibition room devoted to the works of
Diego Rivera.

MUSEO FRANZ MAYER
Av. Hidalgo 45, Centro Histórico, Guerrero, +52 55
5518 2266
www.franzmayer.org.mx
NEIGHBORHOOD: Historic District
ADMISSION: Moderate fee; Tuesdays Free
Occupies the old hospice of the San Juan de Dios
order, this museum is home to Latin America's
largest collection of decorative arts. The museum also
sponsors workshops and temporary exhibitions. Café
located in central garden courtyard.

MUSEO NACIONAL DE ANTROPOLOGIA
Av Paseo de la Reforma y Calzada Gandhi S/N,
Mexico City, +52 55 4040 5300
www.mna.inah.gob.mx
NEIGHBORHOOD: Polanco
This national museum is the most visited museum in
Mexico. Here you'll find significant archaeological
and anthropological artifacts from pre-Columbian
Mexico. Standout pieces include: the Piedra del Sol
(the Aztec calendar stone) and the 16th-century Aztec
statue of Xochipilli. The museum features 23 rooms
of exhibitions filled with pre-Columbian treasures. An
eye-opening collection.

PALACIO NACIONAL
National Palace
Avenida Pino Suarez, Corregidora esquina Guatemala, Zócalo, 52 55 3688 1255
www.hacienda.gob.mx/cultura/museo_virtual_pal_nac/shcp_mv.htm

Of the 150 museums you can visit in Mexico City, this perhaps ought to be your first stop. This building was begun in 1693. The Viceroys of New Spain lived here until the Revolution. They have the whole history of the country's rich cultural diversity on display in the numerous exhibits here. There are huge murals by Diego Rivera depicting the history of the country dating from its pre-Columbian era down through the Mexican Revolution. There's a replica of the first Mexican Congress, Recinto Legislativo. They have English-speaking tour guides.

SOUMAYA MUSEUM
MUSEO SOUMAYA

Blvd. Miguel de Cervantes Saavedra 303, 52 55 1103 9800

www.soumaya.com.mx

NEIGHBORHOOD: Granada

Billionaire Carlos Slim (some years, he's richer than Microsoft's Bill Gates, other years he comes in second or third) put up the money for this great place, which recently moved into a $70 million building, which itself is worth the trip. The Soumaya has the largest collection of Rodin sculptures in Latin America (including more than 350 works by Rodin alone, but that's just part of the 65,000 items Slim donated to the museum, which is named after his late wife). It's better on a weekday if you can manage it because it's less crowded.

SPANISH CULTURAL CENTER

Pasaje Cultural Guatemala 18 — Donceles 97, 55
5521 1925

www.ccemx.org

This Spanish cultural center features art exhibitions,
plays, and music events. (There's a permanent exhibit
of pre-Columbian art and artifacts, as well as rotating
exhibits.) On the weekend (Thurs-Sat) you can see
live music (indie, electronic and rock bands) on the
terrace of the bar-restaurant. In the 1990s, this old
mansion was in ruins until the Spanish government
saved it as a historic monument to the city. The center
hosts workshops, seminars, children's activities,
cultural events and exhibitions.

Chapter 7
SHOPPING & SERVICES

CARLA FERNANDEZ

Av. Álvaro Obregón 200, Mexico City, +52 55 5264 2226

www.carlafernandez.com

NEIGHBORHOOD: Polanco

Carla Fernandez, one of Mexico's top designers, offers her fashions in this boutique. She's known for creating Taller Flora, a demi couture line with a distinct geometric style, co-designed by and using Mexican artisans. Her Pret-a-porter line is also available here. Her fashions have been featured in all the major fashion publications.

CHIC BY ACCIDENT
Lago Texcoco 112, Anáhuac, Mexico City, 52-55-5511-1312

http://chic-by-accident.com

NEIGHBORHOOD: Roma Norte

Designer Emmanuel Picault brings together an exciting and very personal collection of artifacts from different parts of Mexico—furniture, accessories, art pieces, gift items—that will give you a new sense of the richness of the cultural heritage of this country.

COLONIA ROMA
This is one of the older historic neighborhoods in Mexico City that's now packed with shops, boutiques, antique stores, bars and cafes offering a dizzying array of merchandise, art and food. The architectural style is a mix of Art Deco and "Porfirian," a mishmash of styles from Europe fashionable when President Porfirio Díaz was in office. The main streets to focus on are Álvaro Obregón and Calle Colima.

COMMON PEOPLE
Emilio Castelar 149, Mexico City, 52 55 5281 0800
www.commonpeople.com.mx
NEIGHBORHOOD: Polanco
This sociocultural project is filled with unique
collections, the latest trends, valuable objects and
limited editions. It is a concept store that was created
to awaken customer desire for unique and creative
products. Three floors of unique items, many new to
the marketplace, with product testing and creative art,
cuisine, design, and technology.

DULCERIA DE CELAYA
5 de Mayo 39, Mexico City, +52 55 5521 1787
www.dulceriadecelaya.com
NEIGHBORHOOD: Cuauhtémoc
Founded in 1874 and located in an Art Nouveau gem, this is a mecca for lovers of sweets. Here you'll find treats like candied pineapple, guava, and other exotic fruits along with almond paste, candied walnut rolls, and cajeta. Many of these traditional sweets can't be found anywhere else locally.

FABRICA SOCIAL
Calle Isabel la Católica 30, Mexico City, +52 55 5512 0730
www.fabricasocial.org
NEIGHBORHOOD: Historic District
This organization promotes the work of female textile artisans through mobile workshops. This is a great way to bring cultural awareness to communities and sell the work.

GALERÍA DANIEL LIEBSOHN

Londres 161-49, Plaza del Ángel, 52 55 5525 2050
www.liebsohn.com.mx
NEIGHBORHOOD: Juárez
In Daniel's excellent gallery you'll find Mexican and
European antiques mixed with Italian and American
vintage furniture from the 20th century: you may see
a 15th-century Flemish painting beside a lineal seat
by Frank Kyle next to a 19th-century Napoleon III-
style mirror. There's no other gallery like Daniel's in
Mexico City. He has the best taste.

MERCADO DE MEDELLÍN (MARKET MEDELLIN)

Roma Sur, Cuauhtémoc, Mexico City
NEIGHBORHOOD: Distrito Federal
This is a popular Farmers' Market, located on the
corner of Medellin and Campeche, offering a variety
of fresh produce, spices, fresh juices, whole pigs'

heads, meat, and other fresh food items. You'll also find plants, flowers and other items sold in flea market style. This place will give you an idea of the kind of cultural shopping tradition that is being decimated by the arrival of the "supermercados," supermarkets. Closed Sundays.

MERCADO DE JAMAICA
Guillermo Prieto 45, Jamaica, Mexico, +52 55 5741 0002
www.mercadodejamaica.com
NEIGHBORHOOD: Jardín Balbuena
This is a huge flower market that will have your head spinning.

MERCADO DE SAN JUAN
Calle Ernesto Pugibet número 21
www.mercadosanjuan.galeon.com
NEIGHBORHOOD: Centro Poniente
Chefs shop here for foods they later sell you in their restaurants. It's really a unique place where you can get exotic meats like crocodile, ostrich, lion, deer and exotic fruits and vegetables, sweets, spices, meats, cheeses and products it's impossible to find anywhere else. In all probability, you're not there to buy meats and cheeses, but like me, you just want to mix with the local crowds. This is a scene unlike any other. (Great place to buy gift items.) Watch out for pickpockets.

MUSEO TAMAYO
Paseo de la Reforma 51, Mexico City, 52 55 4122 8200
www.museotamayo.org/

NEIGHBORHOOD: Morelos

Not only a great museum but also a great place to purchase art, it's near the National Museum of Anthropology in Chapultepec Park. This museum, run by the Tamayo Foundation, is primarily dedicated to the collection of artist Rufino Tamayo and other contemporary artists like Sophie Calle and Yayoi Kusama.

PANADERÍA ROSETTA (Bakery)

Colima 166, Colonia Roma, Mexico City, 52 55 5207 2976

www.rosetta.com.mx/

NEIGHBORHOOD: Roma Norte

This small bakery offers a variety of classic Mexican baked goods like pan de pulque conchas as well as delicious croissants, and vegan muffins. The menu also includes well-made espresso drinks, sandwiches and house-made pâté.

SANGRE DE MI SANGRE
Orizaba 101, Mexico City, 52 55 5511 8599
www.sdemis.com
NEIGHBORHOOD: Roma Norte
Located in a bohemian neighborhood, this is a
celebration of art and beauty through Sangre de mi
Sangre's jewelry designed by Mariana Villarreal. She
has two lines and her jewelry has been featured in
Vogue, Harper's Bazaar, and Elle magazines.

THE SHOPS AT DOWNTOWN
Isabel La Católica 30, Mexico City
www.theshops.mx
NEIGHBORHOOD: Historic Center
Located in the courtyard of the stately colonial home
of the Counts of Miravalle, built originally in 1846,
is a collection of over 20 unique shops offering food,
crafts, culture and design. The building was saved in
1985 and converted into a commer   cial enterprise.

INDEX

Other Books by the Same Author

Andrew Delaplaine has written in widely varied fields:
screenplays, novels (adult and juvenile), travel writing, journalism. His
books are available in quality bookstores as well as all online retailers.

JACK HOUSTON / ST. CLAIR POLITICAL THRILLERS

THE KEYSTONE FILE – PART 1
THE KEYSTONE FILE – PART 2
THE KEYSTONE FILE – PART 3
THE KEYSTONE FILE – PART 4
THE KEYSTONE FILE – PART 5
THE KEYSTONE FILE – PART 6
THE KEYSTONE FILE – PART 7 *(FINAL)*

On Election night, as China and Russia mass soldiers on their common border
in preparation for war, there's a tie in the Electoral College that forces the
decision for President into the House of Representatives as mandated by the
Constitution. The incumbent Republican President, working through his Aide
for Congressional Liaison, uses the Keystone File, which contains dirt on every
member of Congress, to blackmail members into supporting the Republican
candidate. The action runs from Election Night in November to Inauguration
Day on January 20. Jack Houston St. Clair runs a small detective agency in
Miami. His father is Florida Governor Sam Houston St. Clair, the Republican
candidate. While he tries to help his dad win the election, Jack also gets hired
to follow up on some suspicious wire transfers involving drug smugglers, leading
him to a sunken narco-sub off Key West that has $65 million in cash in its hull.

THE RUNNING MATE

Sam Houston St. Clair has been President for four long years and right now he's bogged down in a nasty fight to be re-elected. A Secret Service agent protecting the opposing candidate discovers that the candidate is sleeping with someone he shouldn't be, and tells his lifelong friend, the President's son Jack, this vital information so Jack can pass it on to help his father win the election. The candidate's wife has also found out about the clandestine affair and plots to kill the lover if her husband wins the election. Jack goes to Washington, and becomes involved in an international whirlpool of intrigue.

AFTER THE OATH: DAY ONE
AFTER THE OATH: MARCH WINDS
WEDDING AT THE WHITE HOUSE

Only three months have passed since Sam Houston St. Clair was sworn in as the new President, but a lot has happened. Returning from Vienna where he met with Russian and Chinese diplomats, Sam is making his way back to Flagler Hall in Miami, his first trip home since being inaugurated. Son Jack is in the midst of turmoil of his own back in Miami, dealing with various dramas, not the least of which is his increasing alienation from Babylon Fuentes and his growing attraction to the seductive Lupe Rodriguez. Fernando Pozo addresses new problems as he struggles to expand Cuba's secret operations in the U.S., made even more difficult as U.S.-Cuban relations thaw. As his father returns home, Jack knows Sam will find as much trouble at home as he did in Vienna.

THE ADVENTURES OF SHERLOCK HOLMES IV

In this series, the original Sherlock Holmes's great-great-great grandson solves crimes and mysteries in the present day, working out of the boutique hotel he owns on South Beach.

THE OKEECHOBEE MURDER

Sherlock Holmes and Watson are called to a remote area of Florida overlooking Lake Okeechobee to investigate a murder where all the evidence points to the victim's son as the killer. Holmes, however, is not so sure.

A MYSTERY IN KEY WEST

Holmes's doctor orders him to take a short holiday in Key West, and while there, Holmes is called on to look into a case in which three people involved in a Santería ritual died with no explanation.

THE CLEVER ONE

A former nun who, while still very devout, has renounced her vows so that she could "find a life, and possibly love, in the real world." She comes to Holmes in hopes that he can find out what happened to the man who promised to marry her, but mysteriously disappeared moments before their wedding.

ENIGMA IN THE REDLANDS

A nanny reaches out to Sherlock Holmes seeking his advice on whether she should take a new position when her prospective employer has demanded that she cut her hair as part of the job.

THE RED-HAIRED MAN

A man with a shock of red hair calls on Sherlock Holmes to solve the mystery of the Red-haired League.

TOO MANY NAPOLEONS

Inspector Lestrade calls on Holmes to help him figure out why a madman would go around Miami breaking into homes and businesses to destroy cheap busts of the French Emperor. It all seems very insignificant to Holmes—until, of course, a murder occurs.

THE MISSING MAN IN THE WINDOW

In what seems to be the case of a missing person, Sherlock Holmes navigates his way through a maze of perplexing clues that leads him through a sinister world to a surprising conclusion.

THE BORNHOLM DIAMOND

A mysterious Swedish nobleman requests a meeting to discuss a matter of such serious importance that it may threaten the line of succession in one of the oldest royal houses in Europe.

SEVERAL TITLES IN THE DELAPLAINE SERIES OF PRE-SCHOOL READERS FOR CHILDREN

THE DELAPLAINE LONG WEEKEND TRAVEL GUIDE SERIES

Delaplaine Travel Guides represent the author's take on some of the many cities he's visited and many of which he has called home (for months or even years) during a lifetime of travel. The books are available as either ebooks or as printed books. Owing to the ease with which material can be uploaded, both the printed and ebook editions are updated 3 times a year.

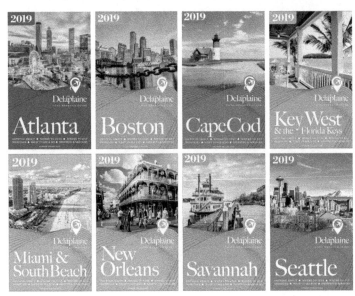

THE FOOD ENTHUSIAST'S
COMPLETE RESTAURANT GUIDES

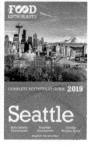